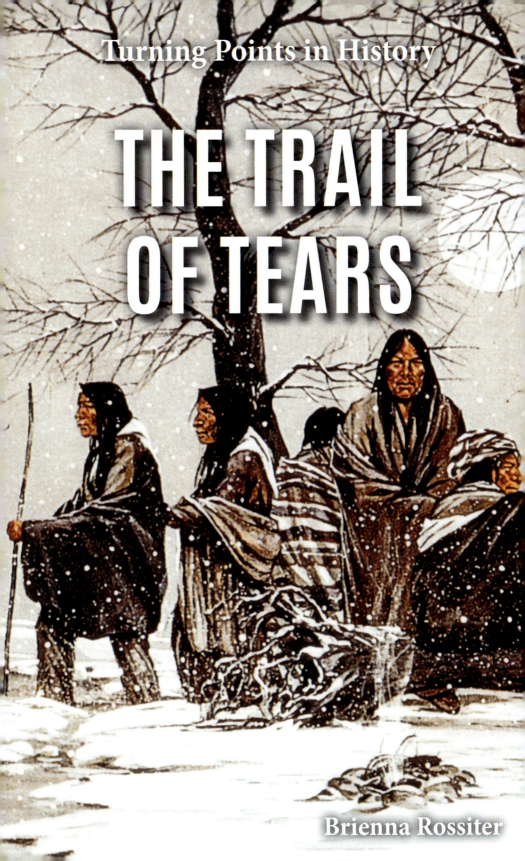

Turning Points in History

THE TRAIL OF TEARS

Brienna Rossiter

WWW.APEXEDITIONS.COM

Copyright © 2025 by Apex Editions, Mendota Heights, MN 55120. All rights reserved. No part of this book may be reproduced or utilized in any form or by any means without written permission from the publisher.

Apex is distributed by North Star Editions:
sales@northstareditions.com | 888-417-0195

Produced for Apex by Red Line Editorial.

Photographs ©: Nativestock.com/Marilyn Angel Wynn, cover, 1; MPI/Archive Photos/Getty Images, 4–5; National Trails Office/National Park Service, 6–7, 39, 40–41, 46–47, 50–51; Picture History/Newscom, 8–9; Robin Rudd/Chattanooga Times Free Press/AP Images, 10–11; National Park Service, 12–13, 22–23, 42–43; National Portrait Gallery/Smithsonian Institution, 14–15, 24, 26–27; Shutterstock Images, 16–17, 34–35, 49, 52–53, 58; Smithsonian American Art Museum, 18–19; North Wind Pictures/Bridgeman Images, 20–21; J. Vespa/WireImage/Getty Images, 25; Library of Congress, 28–29, 30–31, 32–33; Paul Morigi/Smithsonian National Museum of the American Indian/AP Images, 36–37; UIG/Bridgeman Images, 44–45; Pixabay, 54–55; Araya Doheny/Getty Images Entertainment/Getty Images, 56–57

Library of Congress Control Number: 2024944356

ISBN
979-8-89250-465-2 (hardcover)
979-8-89250-481-2 (paperback)
979-8-89250-511-6 (ebook pdf)
979-8-89250-497-3 (hosted ebook)

Printed in the United States of America
Mankato, MN
012025

NOTE TO PARENTS AND EDUCATORS

Apex books are designed to build literacy skills in striving readers. Exciting, high-interest content attracts and holds readers' attention. The text is carefully leveled to allow students to achieve success quickly.

TABLE OF CONTENTS

Chapter 1
FORCED FROM HOME 4

Chapter 2
NATIONS AND TREATIES 10

Chapter 3
REMOVAL RAMPS UP 20

Chapter 4
THE CHEROKEE NEGOTIATE 30

Story Spotlight
ELIAS BOUDINOT 38

Chapter 5
ON THE TRAIL 40

Story Spotlight
TRAIL SURVIVOR 48

Chapter 6
AFTERMATH 50

TIMELINE • 59
COMPREHENSION QUESTIONS • 60
GLOSSARY • 62
TO LEARN MORE • 63
ABOUT THE AUTHOR • 63
INDEX • 64

Chapter 1
FORCED FROM HOME

In 1838, US soldiers entered Cherokee villages. They forced people to leave their homes. Most people had no time to pack. They had to leave most belongings behind.

The United States often used soldiers to force Native nations from their homelands.

The soldiers were there because of a treaty. It said all Cherokee people had to move to Indian Territory. This area was many miles to the west. Many Cherokee people did not want to go there. Soldiers used guns and bayonets to make them leave.

INDIGENOUS REMOVAL

North America is home to hundreds of Indigenous nations. US leaders often wanted their land. So, they would make nations move to new places. Often, these new places had been taken from other Indigenous nations. Some nations were forced to move several times.

In the 1800s, many Cherokee people lived in log cabins.

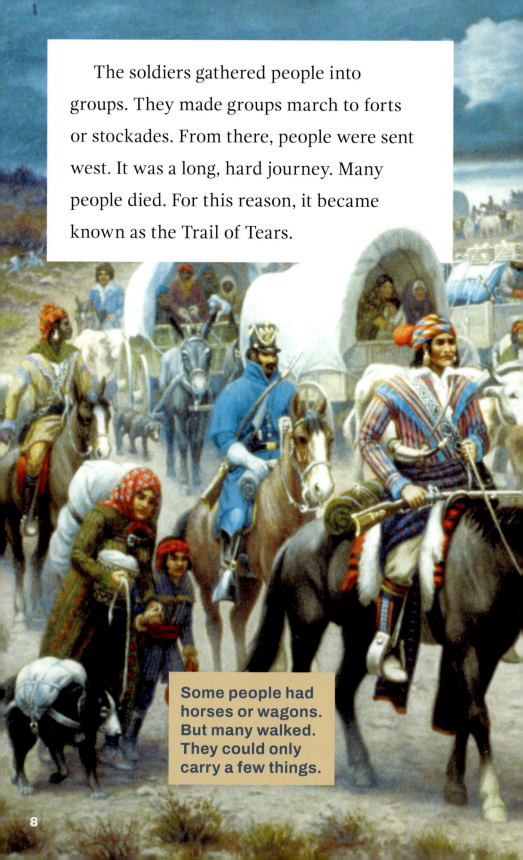

The soldiers gathered people into groups. They made groups march to forts or stockades. From there, people were sent west. It was a long, hard journey. Many people died. For this reason, it became known as the Trail of Tears.

Some people had horses or wagons. But many walked. They could only carry a few things.

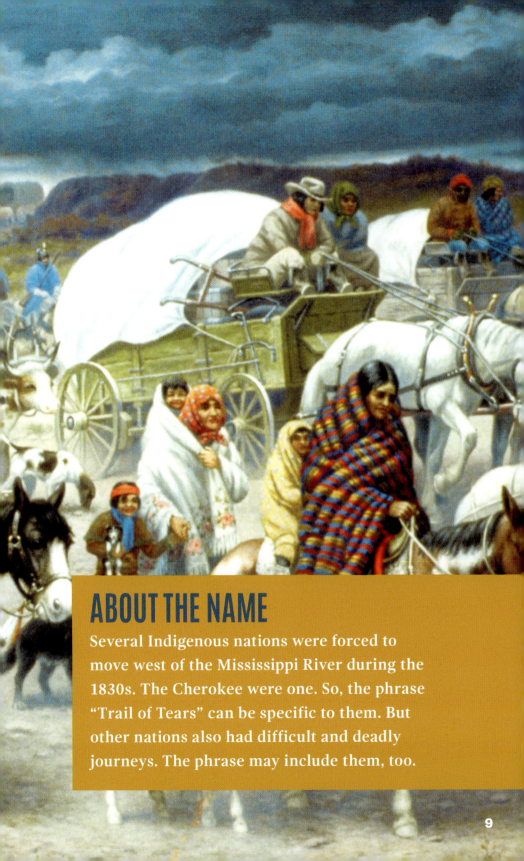

ABOUT THE NAME

Several Indigenous nations were forced to move west of the Mississippi River during the 1830s. The Cherokee were one. So, the phrase "Trail of Tears" can be specific to them. But other nations also had difficult and deadly journeys. The phrase may include them, too.

Chapter 2
NATIONS AND TREATIES

The Trail of Tears forced Indigenous nations to leave the Southeast. It affected thousands of people. Many came from five large Native nations. The Cherokee Nation was one. Others were the Muscogee (Creek), Chickasaw, Choctaw, and Seminole nations.

Today, Cherokee people bike the Trail of Tears every year.

Each nation had its own lands and ways of life. However, white settlers began arriving in the late 1400s. They set up farms and towns.

Some Indigenous groups shared or sold parts of their land. But many resisted. They tried to protect their homelands. Some fought. Others signed treaties. These agreements said where settlers could and couldn't live. However, settlers often broke the treaties. They took over more and more land.

12

The Natchez Trace is a road that has been used for more than 10,000 years. It crosses through traditional Chickasaw, Choctaw, and Natchez lands.

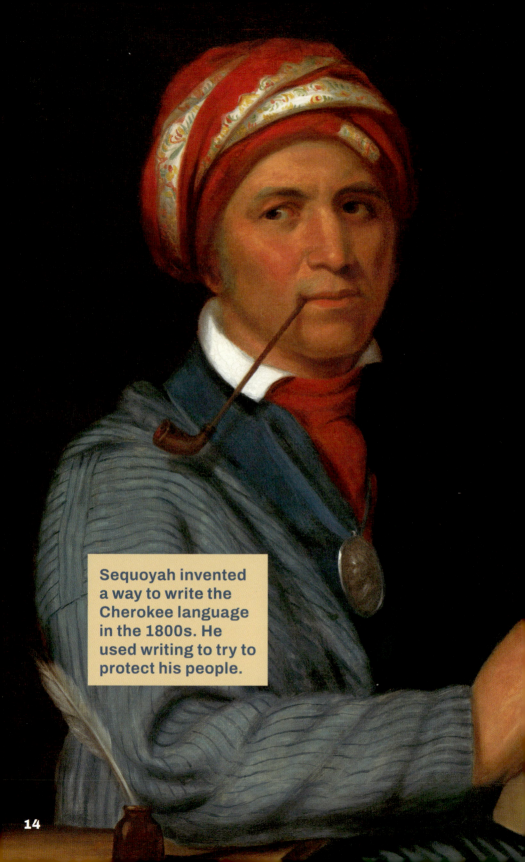

Sequoyah invented a way to write the Cherokee language in the 1800s. He used writing to try to protect his people.

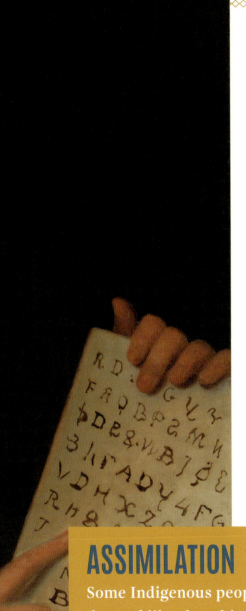

By the 1800s, many US leaders increased their focus on gaining land. This was especially true in Georgia. The state's leaders wanted to make all Indigenous people leave the state. In 1829, people found gold. It was on Cherokee land. Speculators asked Congress to give this land to Georgia.

ASSIMILATION

Some Indigenous people assimilated. They dressed like the white settlers. They spoke English. They grew crops on farms. Many even changed faiths. Some people hoped assimilating would help keep peace with settlers. Often, it did not.

Removing Indigenous people from their land was one of Andrew Jackson's main goals as president.

In 1830, Congress passed the Indian Removal Act. It gave the US president new power. The president could now buy land from Indigenous nations. In return, these nations would move west of the Mississippi River. They would get new land there.

ANDREW JACKSON

Andrew Jackson was the US president from 1829 to 1837. He supported taking Indigenous land. He even helped do it. Between 1814 to 1824, the US government used 11 treaties to get land. Jackson played a key role in nine of them.

Giving up land was supposed to be optional. And many nations were not interested. They loved their homes. Plus, the new land was far away and unfamiliar. Even so, US leaders pressured nations to accept. Eventually, some groups felt they had no choice.

INDIAN TERRITORY

The Indian Removal Act offered land in Indian Territory. This area became part of Oklahoma. But for many years, it was home to Indigenous nations such as the Caddo and Wichita. Other nations had been forced to move there, too. The Osage and Quapaw were two examples.

For hundreds of years, Wichita people lived in villages of grass houses.

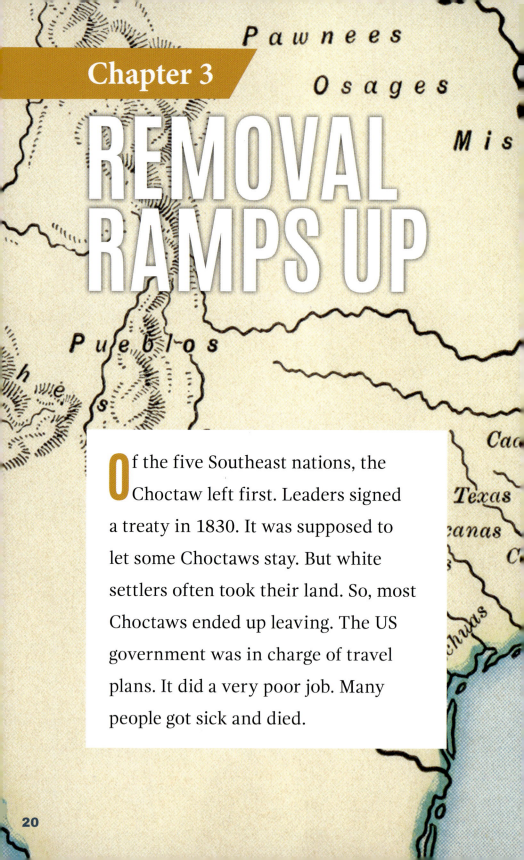

Chapter 3
REMOVAL RAMPS UP

Of the five Southeast nations, the Choctaw left first. Leaders signed a treaty in 1830. It was supposed to let some Choctaws stay. But white settlers often took their land. So, most Choctaws ended up leaving. The US government was in charge of travel plans. It did a very poor job. Many people got sick and died.

The Choctaw were forced to leave their homelands in present-day Mississippi, Alabama, and Louisiana.

The Chickasaw Nation agreed to move west in 1832. But they wanted to manage their own land sales and travel. The US government said it would protect them until they left. It broke this promise. It let white settlers start taking Chickasaw land.

As a result, Chickasaw people began moving in 1837. Careful planning helped their journey go smoother. But other Native nations were in the land they'd been promised. It took further negotiations to get their own space.

Forced removal unsettled Chickasaw villages and ways of life.

The Muscogee signed a different type of treaty in 1832. It allowed settlers to live on part of their land. The rest was supposed to be protected. But settlers started taking that land, too. Some Muscogee people fought back. In response, US leaders ordered all Muscogee people to leave. In 1836, they began their journey. US planners were in charge. Once again, they did a bad job. Many people died.

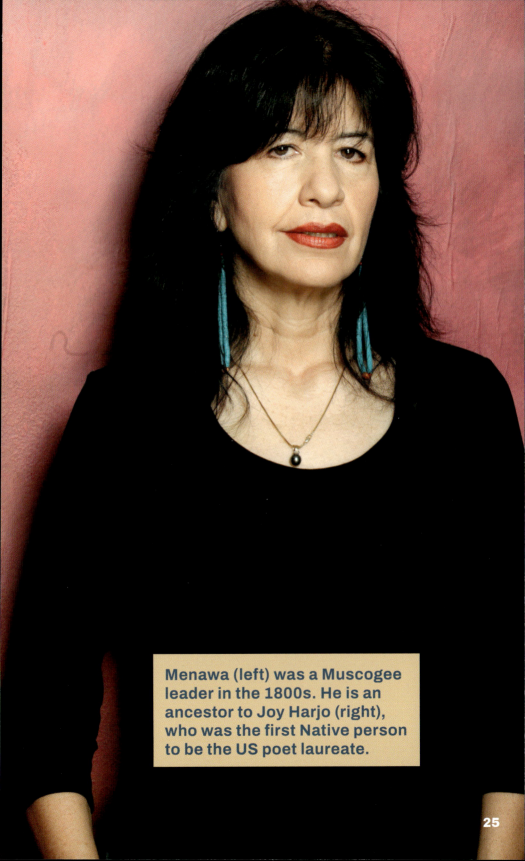

Menawa (left) was a Muscogee leader in the 1800s. He is an ancestor to Joy Harjo (right), who was the first Native person to be the US poet laureate.

Osceola led the Seminoles during the Second Seminole War.

A small group of Seminoles signed a removal treaty in 1833. They were not the Seminole nation's official leaders. So, many Seminole people protested. They said the treaty shouldn't count. US leaders said it did. Many Seminoles refused to leave their homeland in Florida. Fighting broke out. It led to the Second Seminole War.

FIRST SEMINOLE WAR

The First Seminole War took place from 1817 to 1818. The Seminoles had been helping Black people who escaped from slavery. US troops fought to bring these people back. Andrew Jackson helped lead the attacks.

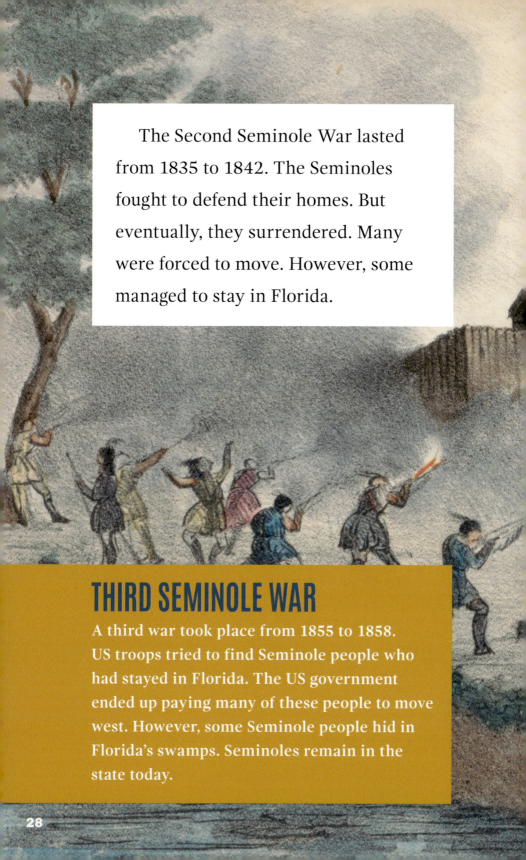

The Second Seminole War lasted from 1835 to 1842. The Seminoles fought to defend their homes. But eventually, they surrendered. Many were forced to move. However, some managed to stay in Florida.

THIRD SEMINOLE WAR

A third war took place from 1855 to 1858. US troops tried to find Seminole people who had stayed in Florida. The US government ended up paying many of these people to move west. However, some Seminole people hid in Florida's swamps. Seminoles remain in the state today.

The Second Seminole War was the longest US war to remove a Native nation.

Chapter 4
THE CHEROKEE NEGOTIATE

At first, the Cherokee Nation resisted removal. They often relied on the law to do so. In 1827, the Cherokee drafted a constitution. It explained their rights as a sovereign nation. One of these rights was owning land.

The Cherokee's constitution was based on the US Constitution.

Cherokee nation. Constitution.

ᏍᏓᏬᎵ, ᎠᏔᎯᎤᎠᏃ

ᎠᏆ ᎾᏛᏅ

ᏃᏍᎦᎣᎠᎧ

ᎾᏛᏴ

ᏣᎳᎩ ᎠᏥᎵ ᏚᎦᎶᎢ

ᎠᏥᎵ ᏚᏍᏲᎢᎢ ᎤᎵᏁᏍ ᏗᏥᏯᏬᎠᎥ.

ᎷᏍ ᏚᏍᏛᎢ:

R. DᏍ T. A. ᎻᏂ, AᏍᎵ DᏂZᏫᏗᎨᏯ, ᏗᏂᎦᏯᎨᏯ, DᏍ ᏍᎸᏆᏍ ᎢᎶᏁᎵ AᏍᎵ,
118 ᏣᎣ ᏍᏫᏗᎶᎢ.

1875.

ᏣᎳᎩ  ᏧᎴᎯ

CHEROKEE PHOENIX

VOL. I.   NEW ECHOTA, THURSDAY APRIL 10, 1828.

EDITED BY ELIAS BOUDINOTT.
PRINTED WEEKLY BY
ISAAC H. HARRIS,
FOR THE CHEROKEE NATION.

At $2.50 if paid in advance, $3 in six months, or $3.50 if paid at the end of the year.

To subscribers who can read only the Cherokee language the price will be $2.00 in advance, or $2,50 to be paid within the year.

Every subscription will be considered as continued unless subscribers give notice to the contrary before the commencement of a new year.

Any person procuring six subscribers, and becoming responsible for the payment, shall receive a seventh gratis.

Advertisements will be inserted at seventy-five cents per square for the first insertion, and thirty-seven and a half cents for each continuance; longer ones in proportion.

☞ All letters addressed to the Editor, post paid, will receive due attention.

AGENTS FOR THE CHEROKEE PHOENIX.

Application has been made to a number of Gentlemen, in different parts of the United States, to act as Agents for this work. We hear, as yet, of only the following who have consented.

Henry Hill, Esq. Treasurer of the A. B. C. F. M. Boston, Mass.
George M. Tracy, Agent of the A. B. C. F. M. New York.
Pollard & Converse,
Rev. James Campbell,
C. L. George Smith,
Besides the above, an itinerant Gentleman, Troy, N. Y. has rendered and will act in future.

CHEROKEE

[CONTINUED]

New Town, ... Resolved by the ... and Council, That any person or persons whatsoever, who shall trade with any negro slave without permission from the proper owner of such slave, and the property so traded for, be proven to have been stolen, the purchaser shall be held and bound to the legal proprietor for the same, or the value thereof; and be it further

Resolved, That any person who shall permit their negro or negroes to purchase spirituous liquors and vend the

---

day for his services during the sitting of the courts.

By order of the National Committee,
JNO. ROSS, Pres't. N. Com.
Approved,
     his
PATH ⨯ KILLER,
     mark.
A. M'COY, Clerk N. Com.
ELIJAH HICKS, Clerk N. Council.

New Town, Nov. 8, 1822.

WHEREAS, the great variety of vices emanating from dissipation, particularly from intoxication, and gaming at cards, which are so prevalent at public places, the national committee and council, seeking the true interest and happiness of their people, have maturely taken this growing evil into their serious consideration, and being fully convinced that no nation of people can prosper and flourish or become magnanimous in character, the basis of whose laws are not founded upon virtue and justice; therefore, to suppress, as much as possible, those demoralizing habits which were introduced by foreign agency.

Resolved by the National Committee That any person or persons whatsoever, who shall bring ardent spirits within three miles of the General council house, or to any of the court houses within the several districts during the general council, or the sitting of the courts, and dispose of the same so as to intoxicate any person or persons whatsoever, the person or persons so offending, shall forfeit his or their whiskey, the same to be destroyed; and be it further

Resolved, That gaming at cards is hereby strictly forbidden, and that any person or persons whatsoever, who ... of fifty dollars each for every such offence, and that any person or persons whatsoever, who shall bring into the Cherokee nation and dispose of playing cards, such person or persons, being convicted before any of the judges, marshals, or light horse, shall pay a fine of twenty-five dollars for every pack of cards so sold; and it shall be the duty of the several judges, marshals and light horse companies to take cognizance of such offences and

---

perior court, to be held at New Town, during the session of each national council, to be composed of the several circuit judges, to determine all causes which may be appealed from the district courts; and

Be it further Resolved, That the law appropriating forty dollars for the support of each district council, is hereby repealed, and that in future the nation shall not be accountable for supplies furnished the district councils.

By order of the National Committee,
JNO. ROSS, Pres't. N. Com.
     his
PATH ⨯ KILLER,
     mark.
ELIJAH HICKS, Clerk N. Com.
A. M'COY, Clerk N. Council.

New Town, Nov. 12, 1822.

Resolved by the National Committee and Council, That the circuit judges be vested with authority to nominate light horse companies in their respective districts, in case of resignation or otherwise, and such nomination being repeated to the head chiefs and sanctioned by them, shall be considered valid.

By order of the N. Committee,
JNO. ROSS, Pres't. N. Com.
Approved—PATH ⨯ KILLER,
A. M'COY, Clerk N. Council.
ELIJAH HICKS, National Com.

New Town, Nov. 13, 1822.

Resolved by the National Committee and Council, That the marshals or tax collectors of the several districts, are hereby authorized to seize upon and attach the property of any person or persons who shall not make punctual payments of their respective taxes, when called upon, and the property so seized and attached shall be advertised ... ten days shall be ... redemption of the property ... In case the property ... turned in that time, ... or collector shall proceed to public sale such ... highest bidder, and all ... which may be received ... of taxes, for which ... be seized, attached ... returned to the person ... from whom it was taken.

By order of the National Com.
JNO ROSS, Pres't. N. Com.
     his
PATH ⨯ KILLER,
A. M'COY, Clerk N. Council.
ELIJAH HICKS, Clerk N. Com.

New Town, Nov. 13, 1822.

Resolved by the National Committee and Council, That the Chattoogee, Chickamauga and other turnpike companies, who have not been heretofore

---

New Town, October ...
Resolved, That the ... council, during the session ... ded on the Sabbaths, ... merchants & pedlars, ... at New Town, close their shops and suspend all any person or persons resolution shall forfeit a ... of fifteen dollars, to be ... the benefit of the nation officer.

By order of the National Com.
JNO. ROSS, Pres't ...
     his
PATH ⨯ KILLER,
     mark.
CHARLES H...
A. McCOY, Sec'y to the ...

New Town, October ...

Resolved by the National and Council, That all ... anating from either body ... the concurrence of the ... the assent and signatories ... chiefs shall be required ... concurrence shall then ... such resolutions.

By order,
JNO. ROSS, P...
Concurred in by the council
     his
PATH ⨯ KIL...
     mark.
A. M'COY, Clerk N. C...
ELIJAH HICKS, C... N...

New Town, Octo...

The National Committee ... that claims of ... ture, which more properly ... to the courts for adjustment ... been taken up by the ... acted upon by that body ... mitted to the Committee ... currence, those claims ... before the committee ... actor of the present ... ties, which makes it ... impossible to investigate ... ters of dispute, therefore

Resolved by the Committee ... matters of private contracts ... before the Council or a ... which have not been acted ... the district courts should ... ted to that court of the ... the parties reside, and ... which have been proper ... decision of the district ... be submitted to the supreme ... session for a decision in ... and equity.

By order,
JNO. ROSS,
     his
Approved—PATH ⨯ KIL...
A. M'COY, Clerk N. Com.
ELIJAH HICKS, Clerk

Georgia's leaders disagreed. They said the Cherokee were not sovereign. They also said Cherokee land was part of the state. Then Georgia passed laws that took away Cherokee rights and property.

In response, the Cherokee sued. In the 1830s, two cases reached the US Supreme Court. Both times, the court agreed with the Cherokee.

However, Georgia's leaders ignored the court. They kept trying to take Cherokee land. And President Jackson let them.

New Echota was the Cherokee's capital city from 1825 to 1838.

In 1835, a group of Cherokee men signed a treaty. It was called the Treaty of New Echota. The signers were not the nation's official leaders. But they said the Cherokee would sell all their land east of the Mississippi River.

Many Cherokee people resisted. They said the men didn't speak for them. They wrote a petition. Thousands signed it. They sent it to US leaders.

A LONG CONTROVERSY

The Treaty of New Echota sparked deep controversy. Some people supported it. They felt the signers were helping their people's long-term survival. Others felt betrayed. People still disagree about the treaty today.

35

The US government honored the treaty. US leaders said the Cherokee had two years to move on their own. Then US soldiers would show up and use force.

ILLEGAL TREATY

Under Cherokee law, all treaties must be signed by consensus. Signing as an individual was illegal. The punishment was death. The signers knew this. In fact, one of them had helped carry out this punishment in the past.

Cherokee people view the Treaty of New Echota at a museum in 2019.

Story Spotlight

ELIAS BOUDINOT

About 500 men signed the treaty at New Echota. Elias Boudinot was one of them. At first, he was against relocating. But he later changed his mind. Boudinot worked for a newspaper. In the 1830s, he wrote several articles. They explained his change in thinking. He felt the US government would not give up. So, people had to find a way to survive.

Later, Boudinot and two other signers were killed. This was for breaking Cherokee law by signing.

> Elias Boudinot helped start the *Cherokee Phoenix*. He also raised money for its printing press.

Chapter 5

ON THE TRAIL

By 1838, about 2,000 Cherokee people had migrated. The other 16,000 stayed. So, the US government sent 7,000 soldiers to make them move. Troops rounded up people from throughout Georgia, Alabama, Tennessee, and North Carolina.

In 1837, Cherokee leaders met at their council house in what is now Cleveland, Tennessee. They learned there that removal would happen.

Soldiers brought Cherokee people to stockades. The camps were in or near Tennessee. Then the soldiers divided people into batches. Each batch would head west at a different time. Until then, people waited in crowded stockades. Some people stayed there for weeks. Sickness spread easily. Many people died.

Stockades were often made quickly with logs.

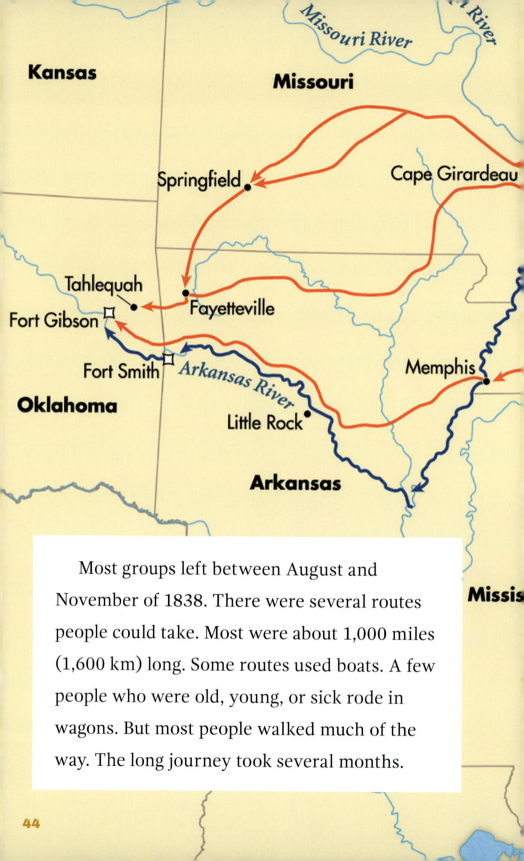

Most groups left between August and November of 1838. There were several routes people could take. Most were about 1,000 miles (1,600 km) long. Some routes used boats. A few people who were old, young, or sick rode in wagons. But most people walked much of the way. The long journey took several months.

44

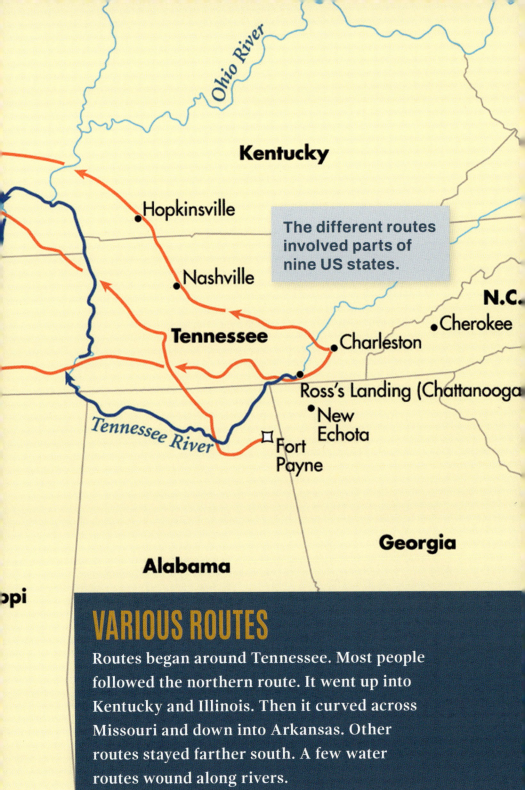

The different routes involved parts of nine US states.

VARIOUS ROUTES

Routes began around Tennessee. Most people followed the northern route. It went up into Kentucky and Illinois. Then it curved across Missouri and down into Arkansas. Other routes stayed farther south. A few water routes wound along rivers.

Travelers faced terrible conditions. People didn't have enough food. They traveled for months. Then a cold winter hit early. People had only rough camps for shelter. Thousands froze or starved to death.

By March 1839, all groups had reached the new land. They built new homes and lives. But they had few supplies. And many were ill from the long, hard journey.

MANTLE ROCK

People stopped at camps to rest or wait out bad weather. One camp was at Mantle Rock. People waited there to cross the Ohio River. But the last group got stuck. Cold weather froze the river. People died while waiting.

Many people had to wait for a ferry at Lake Dardanelle in Russellville, Arkansas.

Story Spotlight

TRAIL SURVIVOR

Sallie Farney survived the Trail of Tears. Her family was Muscogee. Soldiers brought them to a stockade. Then they had to walk for miles. Farney's grandfather died on the trail. So did many others. There was little time to bury them. But people encouraged one another to keep going despite the hardship.

Farney told this story to her granddaughter Mary Hill. Hill retold it in 1937. Today, Muscogee people keep these kinds of stories alive. That way, more people can understand the past.

There are more than 120,000 Muscogee Nation citizens today.

49

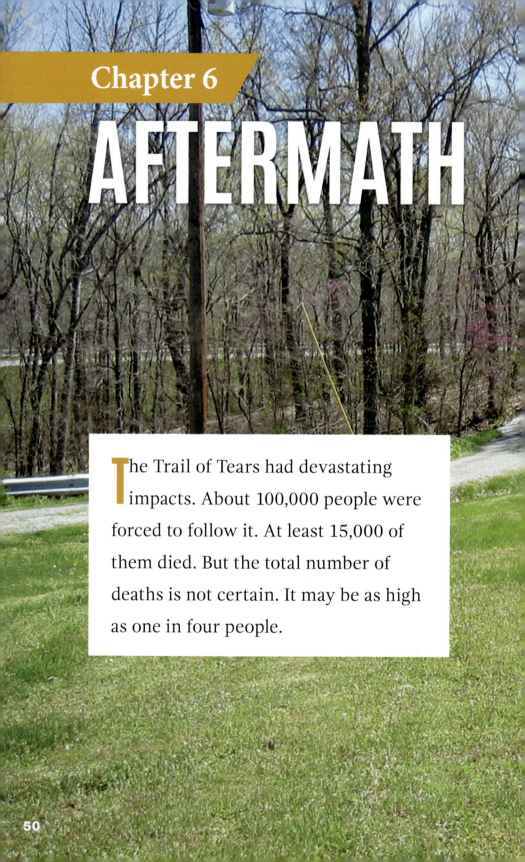

Chapter 6

AFTERMATH

The Trail of Tears had devastating impacts. About 100,000 people were forced to follow it. At least 15,000 of them died. But the total number of deaths is not certain. It may be as high as one in four people.

For the Cherokee alone, experts estimate that 4,000 or more people died on the Trail of Tears. Elders and children were especially likely to die.

Many deaths were caused by cold, sickness, or lack of food. More supplies and better planning could have prevented this from happening. But US leaders failed to provide these things. Some leaders did so on purpose. In fact, removal has been called "ethnic cleansing."

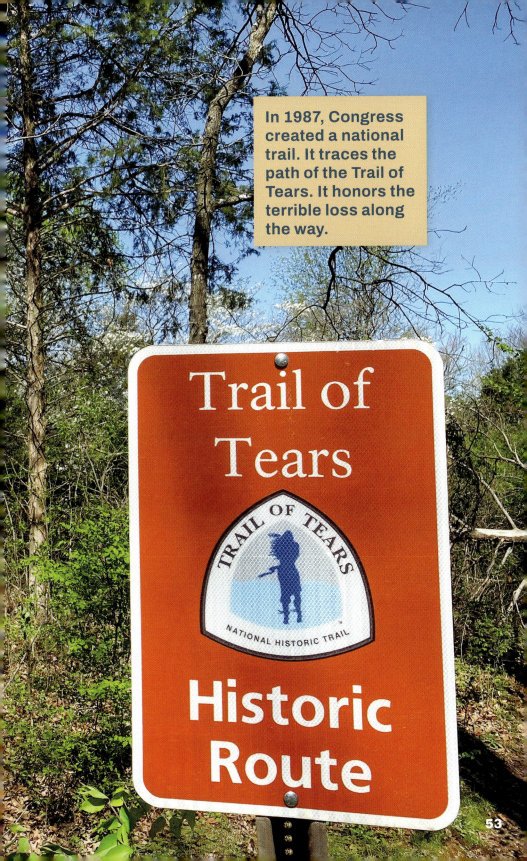
In 1987, Congress created a national trail. It traces the path of the Trail of Tears. It honors the terrible loss along the way.

Despite the harm, the trail's survivors built new lives. Like before, tribes governed themselves. They formed their own schools, courts, and laws.

In 1907, Oklahoma became a state. In the years leading up to that, US leaders changed how land was owned. They gave it to individuals instead of tribes. This made land easier for settlers to take. Some bought it. Others used tricks.

RAILROAD RUSH

In the 1860s, the Transcontinental Railroad was built across the United States. It went through Indian Territory. Settlers rushed to the area. More removals took place. In the 1890s, some nations were pushed farther west.

In 1847, the Choctaw were still recovering from the Trail of Tears. Even so, they donated money to the Irish when many were starving. In 2017, the Irish built a sculpture to honor that gift.

The TV show *Reservation Dogs* was filmed in the Muscogee Nation. It features scenes about the Trail of Tears.

NOT LEAVING

About 1,000 Cherokee people managed not to relocate. They stayed in North Carolina. Sixty families got permission to stay. And a few hundred people hid in the mountains. Still others returned after completing the trail. As a result, more than 14,000 Cherokee people live in this area today. They are known as the Eastern Band of Cherokee Indians.

Nevertheless, many Indigenous people kept their land and ways of life. Tribal governments continue today. So do traditions and cultures.

People have also built museums and memorials along the trail. They help people learn about those who died.

TIMELINE

MAY 1830 — Congress passes the Indian Removal Act, which President Andrew Jackson signs into law.

SEPTEMBER 27, 1830 — The Choctaw Nation signs a treaty that leads to their removal.

MARCH 24, 1832 — The Muscogee (Creek) Nation signs a treaty that gives up part of their land.

OCTOBER 20, 1832 — Members of the Chickasaw Nation sign a treaty agreeing to leave their homeland.

DECEMBER 28, 1835 — The Second Seminole War breaks out after US leaders honor a treaty made by a group who were not the nation's official leaders.

DECEMBER 29, 1835 — A group of Cherokee men signs the Treaty at New Echota.

MAY 26, 1838 — US soldiers begin rounding up Cherokee people and forcing them to march west.

MARCH 1839 — The last group of Cherokee people from the Southeast reaches Indian Territory.

COMPREHENSION QUESTIONS

Write your answers on a separate piece of paper.

1. Write a few sentences describing how the phrase "Trail of Tears" is typically used.

2. Which way of resisting removal did you think was most likely to work? Why?

3. Which of the following nations was the first to move west?

    A. the Choctaw
    B. the Chickasaw
    C. the Seminoles

4. Where are Cherokee governments located today?

    A. only in Oklahoma
    B. only in North Carolina
    C. in both Oklahoma and North Carolina

5. What does **protested** mean in this book?

*So, many Seminole people **protested**. They said the treaty shouldn't count.*

    A. said something was not fair or right
    B. agreed with a person or idea
    C. planned a surprise attack on an enemy

6. What does **migrated** mean in this book?

*By 1838, about 2,000 Cherokee people had **migrated**. The other 16,000 stayed.*

    A. changed their minds
    B. remained where they were
    C. moved to a new place

Answer key on page 64.

GLOSSARY

assimilated
Lived like most other Americans.

bayonets
Sharp blades that stick out from the ends of guns.

consensus
Agreement from most people in a group.

ethnic cleansing
Purposely killing or sending away a particular group of people.

Indigenous
Related to the original people who lived in an area.

negotiations
Meetings in which people try to solve a problem or reach an official agreement.

petition
A formal request that many people sign and send to a leader.

sovereign
In control of itself, and not under another country's rule or laws.

speculators
People who tried to earn lots of money by finding and selling gold.

stockades
Buildings made from wood posts, often used to hold soldiers or prisoners.

treaty
An agreement between countries or groups.

TO LEARN MORE
BOOKS

Bird, F. A. *Cherokee*. Minneapolis: Abdo Publishing, 2022.

DeGroat, Cayla Bellanger. *Indigenous Cultures Today: Protecting Native Families and Practicing Cultural Traditions*. Minneapolis: Lerner Publications, 2025.

Harris, Duchess, with Kate Conley. *The Indian Removal Act and the Trail of Tears*. Minneapolis: Abdo Publishing, 2020.

ONLINE RESOURCES

Visit **www.apexeditions.com** to find links and resources related to this title.

ABOUT THE AUTHOR

Brienna Rossiter is a writer and editor who lives in Minnesota.

INDEX

Alabama, 40

Boudinot, Elias, 38

Caddo, 18
Chickasaw, 10, 22
Choctaw, 10, 20

Eastern Band of Cherokee Indians, 56

Farney, Sallie, 48
Florida, 27–28

Georgia, 15, 33, 40

Indian Removal Act, 17–18
Indian Territory, 6, 18, 54

Jackson, Andrew, 17, 27, 33

Mantle Rock, 47
Mississippi River, 9, 17, 35
Muscogee (Creek), 10, 24, 48

North Carolina, 40, 56

Oklahoma, 18, 54
Osage, 18

Quapaw, 18

Seminoles, 10, 27–28
Seminole Wars, 27–28
settlers, 12, 15, 20, 22, 24, 54
sickness, 20, 42, 44, 52
stockades, 8, 42, 48

Tennessee, 40, 42, 45
treaties, 6, 12, 17, 20, 24, 27, 35–36, 38
Treaty of New Echota, 35–36, 38

US soldiers, 4, 6, 8, 36, 40, 42, 48
US Supreme Court, 33

Wichita, 18

ANSWER KEY:
1. Answers will vary; 2. Answers will vary; 3. A; 4. C; 5. A; 6. C